How-To Guides for Fiendish Rulers

A King's Guide

Thanks to the creative team:
Senior Editor: Alice Peebles
Consultant: John Haywood
Fact Checker: Kate Mitchell
Design: www.collaborate.agency

Hungry Tomato™
A division of Lerner Publishing Group, Inc.
241 First Avenue North
Minneapolis, MN 55401 USA

For reading levels and more information, look up
this title at www.lernerbooks.com.

Main body text set in Blokletters Balpen 9/13.
Typeface provided by LeFly Fonts.

Library of Congress Cataloging-in-Publication Data

Names: Chambers, Catherine, 1954- author. | Pentney, Ryan, illustrator.
Title: A King's Guide / Catherine Chambers ; Illustrated by Ryan Pentney.
Description: Original Edition. | Minneapolis : Hungry Tomato, 2016. |
Series: How-To Guides for Fiendish Rulers | Includes index. |
Audience: Grades 4 to 6.
Identifiers: LCCN 2016021981 (print) | LCCN 2016025120 (ebook) | ISBN
9781512415506 (library bound : alk. paper) | ISBN 9781512430721 (pbk. :
alk. paper) | ISBN 9781512427066 (eb pdf)
Subjects: LCSH: Europe—Kings and rulers—History—To 1500—Juvenile
literature. | Middle Ages—Juvenile literature. | Castles—Europe—History—To
1500—Juvenile literature. | Battles—Europe—History—To 1500—Juvenile
literature. | Europe—History—476-1492—Juvenile literature.
Classification: LCC D107 .C49 2016 (print) | LCC D107 (ebook) | DDC
321/.60940902—dc23

LC record available at https://lccn.loc.gov/2016021981

Manufactured in the United States of America
1-39910-21380-8/10/2016

How-To Guides for Fiendish Rulers

A King's Guide

by Catherine Chambers
Illustrated by Ryan Pentney

HUNGRY
TOMATO.

CONTENTS

Writing Down My Rules

I am a very fiendish medieval king. I have ruled my kingdom for many years. I am very successful but am no longer young. So I need to write down my rules for my son. If he follows them, he will become as great as me. Well, almost.

MY RULES MUST BE PLAIN AND CLEAR. So I have asked a trusted abbot to pick his most skilled monks to write my rules. They pull out sheets of the smoothest vellum made of tender lambskin. Then they dip their fine goose quill pens into inkhorns. They bend over their sloped desks, and the work begins. I see a mistake—already! The abbot rubs it out carefully with a piece of pumice stone.

WILL I DIE BEFORE MY RULEBOOK IS COMPLETE?
I feel quite sick with worry. My courtier sends for the astrologer. He hurries along with my star chart but says that my future is uncertain. I am carried to my four-poster bed feeling miserable.
I wait for a doctor.

KEEP WRITING THOSE RULES!
The monks are now working here in my vast bedchamber. They squint in the firelight, so I order my best beeswax candles to be lit. The doctor arrives. He sees me quivering. Maybe I am having a seizure. I might need trepanning—having a hole drilled in my skull to relieve my illness. NOOO!

I DEMAND TO KNOW THE TRUTH. Can I be cured? The doctor says that I do not need trepanning. Phew! But he decides that my spirits are low—my blood must have too much black bile. This causes melancholia, or sadness. He suggests leeches to draw out blood and restore the balance in my body. I am relieved. I will need to lose quite a lot of blood, the doctor tells me. The monks smile. How very kind. "NOW GET BACK TO WORK!" I tell them. And they do.

The ink on the last sheet is drying. My rules are complete. Here they are. I hope my son follows them. He must!

How to Become a Medieval King

I followed rule number one and became king when my father died. I share this rule with most medieval kingdoms from Eastern Europe to England in the far west. Of course, the oldest son should take over. But younger sons sometimes get there first, with the help of scheming nobles and a battle. Actually, I am not my father's oldest son, so I did bend the rules a little.

I only rule a bit of it—but just you wait!

Because you stole his chess pieces when he was six.

I INSIST I AM THE BEST PERSON FOR THE JOB. My nobles agree. My older brother was away fighting when my father died. I took my chance and declared myself king. My brother is still fighting—to get back into the country! My best knights are on the borders, keeping him out. And just to be extra-safe, I think I might also send my brother's sons very far away. Or arrange for them to die. I will make it look like I am totally innocent, of course.
I care about my reputation.

SOME NOBLE FAMILIES REFUSE TO STICK TO THE RULES. My family dynasty, or line of descent, goes back many generations. But in some kingdoms, a new powerful family sometimes takes over and creates a new dynasty. I learn a lot from other countries about how this might happen. It makes me shudder!

> I support you because you always do what I say.

I MUST KEEP AN EYE ON MY WIFE. I get very nervous when I think of Eleanor (1122–1204), Queen of England and parts of France. She became Queen when her husband became King Henry II (1133–1189). Eleanor supported him for twenty years, until . . . she plotted with two of her favorite sons to overthrow him! Luckily, I am my mother's favorite son, which is partly why I am now King. I suppose I shouldn't complain about strong wives and mothers.

Fiendish Fact File

• The medieval period is also known as the Middle Ages. Historians date this from the fifth to the fifteenth centuries CE. A lot changed in that time!

• Queen Eleanor was strong and clever. She arranged marriages between her children and French royalty, which increased England's power in France.

Strangely, some kings share power with their brothers! **BUT I WILL NOT ALLOW POWER SHARING.** Princes from the early medieval German Habsburg Empire (1282–1379) and Sweden made agreements to share their domains, the lands under their control. Terrible idea!

My Power Comes from God

Yes, that's right. God's rule says I'm in charge of my kingdom. You cannot get more powerful than that. But God also gave power to our religious leaders, especially the Pope. He is the head of the mighty Roman Catholic Church. They tax the peasants on their lands so much that they are wealthier than ME!

EVERYONE MUST BOW AND SCRAPE. They must bow as they enter my chamber and leave walking backward, still bowing. They should never turn their backs on me. I mean, would you turn your back on a king blessed by God? Even my powerful bishops bow to me. I protect them, but I keep my eye on them. Their friendships with bishops in other kingdoms trouble me. I need their support. Fortunately, they need mine too. It's like a balancing act.

I'm God's bestest friend.

I MUST BUILD BEAUTIFUL CHAPELS. My subjects are happy to see me spending money building chapels. There priests and monks will pray for my soul and my kingdom. These prayers make my subjects feel very protected by God and loyal to ME. My chapels have beautifully painted walls and ceilings, tiles glazed with my coat of arms, and bright stained glass windows.

> If only I had a great big cathedral instead of this tiny chapel.

I ALLOW MY BISHOPS TO BUILD GREAT CATHEDRALS. Actually, I cannot stop them. They have so much money and support from the Pope. But at least I was crowned in our biggest, grandest cathedral, showing my God-given status. Such pomp and ceremony! A bishop even marked my head with holy oil, just like they would a priest. This is excellent—people are too scared to murder priests, so hopefully they will not murder ME.

I MUST RESPECT HAPPY HOLY DAYS. This is a dreadful rule, but I just have to accept it. The church grants my lowly peasants holy days—or holidays! Most holidays celebrate saints (lots of them), and my subjects join in processions, pageants, and games. They pray to a saint's relics (teeth, bones, or hair) as a way of asking God to cure their diseases. My subjects can buy relics too. But are they real? I need a rule about false relics.

> I've bought three thumbs belonging to Saint Nigel.

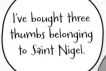

Fiendish Fact File

• Medieval German stonemasons began building the great church Ulm Minster in 1377. It was not completed until 1890! It is the tallest church in the world.

• Tensions often erupted between kings and bishops. Henry II of England (1133–1189) had his Archbishop, Thomas Becket (about 1118–1170), murdered in Canterbury Cathedral.

My Scheming Court

I've finished all the jobs in a week, and he's not back for another year.

I wish I could rule with ministers who will never betray me. But this is unlikely. My Chief Justice Minister is also my Viceroy, and he runs the country when I am away. Very scary. Sometimes my Queen takes over many functions for me. I THINK I can trust her.

I WILL HIRE AND FIRE ALL MINISTERS. My ministers advise me about money, taxes, law, and much more. Some are my brothers, the dukes. Others are counts from very ancient and horribly powerful families. They are not of royal blood, but I can't seem to get rid of them. I choose the best of them to be the Treasurer, the Constable in charge of my army, and the Master of the Horse, who runs the royal stables. He looks after all my events and visits too, which are planned to make me look just BRILLIANT.

I MUST SAVE MY DARKEST SECRETS FOR MY SMALLEST ROOM. My closest companion and official works in my bathroom. Some say that flushing away filthy water is a lowly job. But I choose my Groom of the Stool to discuss the most important matters in the most private room in the palace. Other members of my household and government fear his power. At times, I confess, so do I.

Your secret really stinks, My Lord King.

12

I CHOOSE MY OWN FRIENDS —CAREFULLY. I do like to laugh and joust with a few friends. Most of them are vassal knights and sons of lords. We had such fun growing up together when they were court pageboys and I was a spoiled prince. As seven-year-olds we practiced hunting and fencing skills. Of course they let me win, and they still do. I gave them fiefdoms, which are tracts of land with lots of tax-paying peasants.

NOBLES! I KEEP AN EYE ON YOU! I use my royal couriers to deliver messages to my nobles—and spy on them. My messages are usually given by word of mouth, leaving no evidence. In any case, most of my subjects cannot read or write. My favorite courier has to ask a priest to help him read any written message. But can I trust the priest?

Fiendish Fact File

- Priests called confessors heard a king's confessions of his sins. They were sworn to secrecy, but a king probably didn't admit his worst sins until he was on his deathbed!

- A king might die when his son was a child. Then regents—ministers or other princes—would make decisions for the infant king. But they weren't always fair.

It says, "The King wants you to tell the count that you're really a spy."

How I Keep Law and Order

There is no point being soft, so I operate a tough court system. I do not care much about crimes in villages. These are mostly drunken brawls and petty theft. So their vassal lords deal with them in manor courts. However, treason, spying, poaching my deer, or cutting down my trees must be sorted out in my royal courts, by ME.

I AIM TO TERRIFY MY NOBLES. I tell my nobles to sort out their constant arguing with duels. The innocent will win, of course. A noble who seems at fault might be forced to eat a thick slice of bread in one gulp. If he chokes, then we know he's guilty. Be warned, my nobles! I will have you hanged, beheaded, or worse if you betray me.

I'm better-fed here than at home.

GOD WILL JUDGE POOR PETTY CRIMINALS . . . after they are tested through trial by ordeal. The accused holds a rod of red-hot iron, and if the burn does not heal in three days, he is guilty. His hands, feet, and head are jammed in the stocks for days. Passersby throw muck or rotten food at him. A cruel rule—but I like it.

Stand up straight, man!

MY BACKSTABBING ENEMIES WILL ROT IN JAIL. I imprison them in the Great Keep, which is the strongest part of the castle. Truly treacherous enemies are dumped in the oubliette, a deep opening set in the castle wall. The word comes from the French for "to forget." Here, the prisoner only has room to stand up, and he is soon forgotten. After a while, his body is hauled up with a rope.

I STILL CANNOT FORCE MY RULES ON THE BISHOPS. My lord bishops tell me that my torture methods are too cruel. But I hear they torture people too! And they make peasants pay them one-tenth of their harvest. This is a tax called a tithe, to support the church. The peasants take their tithes to tithe barns even if times are hard. That's a real crime.

Fiendish Fact File
- Kings often kidnapped their noble enemies' children. But they were allowed to play in the castle grounds.
- Some torture instruments were portable, such as thumbscrews, which slowly crushed fingers and thumbs.

Ouch!

15

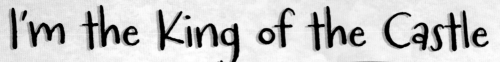

I'm the King of the Castle

My enormous castles are a symbol of power. They look really terrifying on top of a cliff, the mouth of a seaport, or a bend in a river. They protect my trade routes too. I enjoy defending my castles by showering down arrows, boiling tar, and worse on my enemies. That's the fun part. In peacetime I run my kingdom from the castles, giving orders and collecting taxes.

I'm off. The last time they threw urine at me, it bleached my flag.

I DEMAND THE THICKEST WALLS IN

EUROPE! I build most of my castles around a tall, solid rock. The turrets are linked by stone walls more than 20 feet (6 meters) thick. Inside, the central square is framed by a network of solid chambers, my chapel, and a large, grand hall. We've come a long way from the castles of my ancestors, which were just turrets mostly made of wood. Pathetic.

Where's the door? I said a thick wall, not a solid wall!'

YOU WILL NOT GET IN! *If an enemy thinks he can climb the walls, he should think twice. They are surrounded by a deep moat full of water and sharp spikes. At an enemy's approach, I order the drawbridge to be pulled up. If he does step on it (unlikely), he'll get tossed in the moat!*

Er—where do we go from here?

I MUST KEEP ORDER WITHIN MY CASTLE WALLS.
But it's a nightmare. Hundreds of people live here. Some set up market stalls. Others even herd pigs and raise chickens to provide my kitchens with meat and eggs. If my lands are threatened, I open up my castle to nearby villagers. That's even more of a nightmare. But I usually make an agreement with my enemy so that a siege doesn't happen. A fiendishly clever rule.

I INSIST ON GOOD HYGIENE.
Our personal wastewater shoots through holes in wooden seats. Then it gushes straight down the outside of the castle walls and into a cesspit or the moat below. In summer this creates an absolute stink.

Fiendish Fact File

- Turret staircases were built up clockwise. Most soldiers held their swords in their right hands, so intruders would hit their swords on the walls as they fought to the top.

- Peasants lived in two-roomed houses made of a wooden frame covered with mud, straw, and animal dung.

Being a Bad Neighbor

I do try to sort out disputes with other kingdoms through their diplomats. But not for long. I soon send in the troops. One of my goals is to expand my kingdom. I like grabbing domains close by, so trusted nobles and knights can keep an eye on them. Sometimes I have to defend my borders from neighbors trying to attack ME!

You've got three minutes to explain your king's position—then run for your lives!

But Your Majesty, our King only wants to be your friend!

I'LL TRAVEL FAR FOR A GOOD FIGHT. I have led my army all the way to Palestine in the Middle East to attack Jerusalem. At the moment, a great Muslim leader called Saladin rules it. He is so powerful that I have to fight alongside my European rivals! We call this war the Crusades, and it's very tough. But my subjects will respect me for defending our faith. We have won a lot of territory so far and have opened up trade in the Mediterranean. That means spices, silks, and other good stuff—a just reward.

I MUST FIND OUT WHO ARE MY REAL ENEMIES. I mean, I don't want to end up like England's Richard I (1157-1199). He took his army to Jerusalem but eventually made a friendly truce with Saladin. On the way back, he was captured in Venice by Duke Leopold V of Austria (1157-1194). I thought they were best friends.

MY FIENDISH RULES ON TRADE.

1. Tax the merchants.
2. Charge tolls on bridges along trade routes.
3. Make towns pay for special rights to trade.

I am very keen to find out the rules of the Hanseatic League. This group of cities in northern Europe seems to have been rich FOREVER (since the thirteenth century)! They have their own soldiers—but no kings!

Actually, that is a scary thought.

> Who needs a king? They're expensive, and they only cause trouble.

I MUST FIND MORE MONEY FOR MY BATTLES. My army is very expensive, especially when I fight abroad and have to pay foreign mercenary knights. To get money and supplies, I ask for tribute from defeated towns and villages. In return, I promise that my troops won't loot their homes or take their livestock and crops. I am so kind.

Fiendish Fact File

- Czech King Jan of Luxembourg (1296-1346) joined the bloody Battle of Crécy between France and England even though he was blind. He died on the battlefield.

- The Hundred Years War between the English and French lasted more than a century (1337-1453).

> No, I've never owned a cow. Honestly!

I Lead from the Front

Pleeease come and fight—I promise no taxes for ten years. Twenty?

I cannot afford to look like a coward. So I insist on leading my army into battle. My knights gather together their best professional archers, both freedmen and peasants, to help out. But unbelievably, some of them refuse! They say they need to work on the farm. What is the point of being King if I cannot enforce my rules?

I INSIST ON THE BIGGEST FIGHTING MACHINES. I attack my enemy's positions, or their castles, with ballistas, a kind of giant crossbow, and great catapults called trebuchets. These shoot massive stones, explosives, hot bolts of iron, and even diseased bodies at the enemy. We aim up and over the ramparts. Then our archers move in. A hundred or more soldiers wheel in the siege towers. Time for my soldiers to climb up and take over!

Fiendish Fact File

- The morning star was a club with a round metal head covered in spikes. It was used by both infantry and cavalry.

- A steel war hammer's pick end could cause concussion without piercing the helmet.

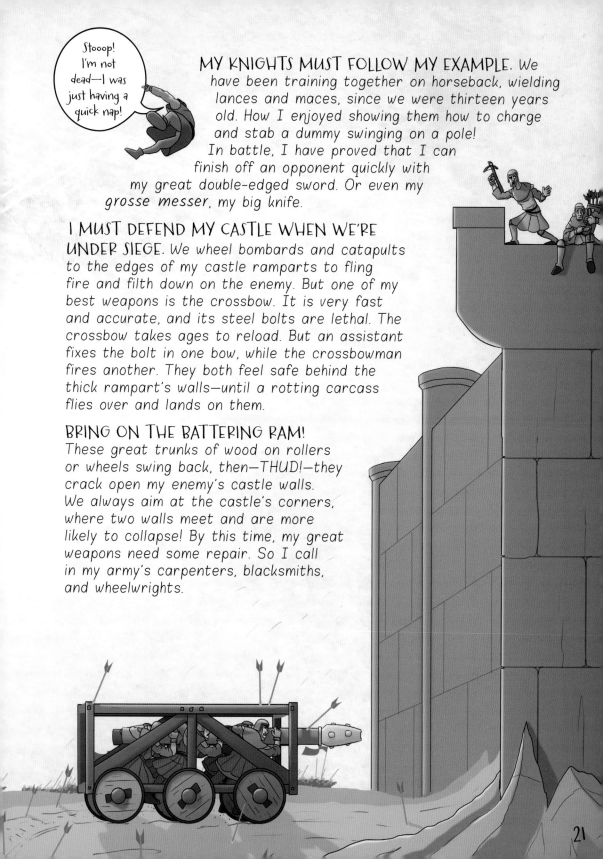

Stooop! I'm not dead—I was just having a quick nap!

MY KNIGHTS MUST FOLLOW MY EXAMPLE. We have been training together on horseback, wielding lances and maces, since we were thirteen years old. How I enjoyed showing them how to charge and stab a dummy swinging on a pole! In battle, I have proved that I can finish off an opponent quickly with my great double-edged sword. Or even my *grosse messer*, my big knife.

I MUST DEFEND MY CASTLE WHEN WE'RE UNDER SIEGE. We wheel bombards and catapults to the edges of my castle ramparts to fling fire and filth down on the enemy. But one of my best weapons is the crossbow. It is very fast and accurate, and its steel bolts are lethal. The crossbow takes ages to reload. But an assistant fixes the bolt in one bow, while the crossbowman fires another. They both feel safe behind the thick rampart's walls—until a rotting carcass flies over and lands on them.

BRING ON THE BATTERING RAM!
These great trunks of wood on rollers or wheels swing back, then—THUD!—they crack open my enemy's castle walls. We always aim at the castle's corners, where two walls meet and are more likely to collapse! By this time, my great weapons need some repair. So I call in my army's carpenters, blacksmiths, and wheelwrights.

Looking Rich, Famous, and Intelligent

I should have listened to my Latin teacher. Nice pictures though.

Even on the battlefield it is obvious who I am as I wear my crown over my helmet. I insist that my page make my armor shine, especially the shield emblazoned with my coat of arms. A flag bearer rides by my side, waving my heraldic standard. At home, all is luxury. I show off my books made from the best vellum, or skins, and decorated with gold leaf paint. They make me seem clever.

MY COURT IS A HUB OF ENTERTAINMENT. My noble guests hear the finest bas musical instruments. These are quiet and refined and do not bellow like the haut instruments of the streets. No, my court is filled with the sound of harps, lutes, and the dulcimer, with its fine wires struck by soft hammers. As they play, a bard tells tales of my good and daring deeds. Of course, at times I just want a bit of fun. Then I call in jesters, jugglers, acrobats, and clowns.

I saw you fight with all your might. Oh, sorry! That's a mistake. It was your knight.

GOLD RULES! Gold, silver, sapphires, and rubies—I have them all. Not to mention caskets of coins. My jewels are not cut but polished. So they glow rather than dazzle. They are set in gold with enamel designs made from shiny colored glass burned onto them. My lesser lords have to deal with jewelry made of copper and pewter—not nearly as nice.

I MUST NOT APPEAR IGNORANT. *Kings who know nothing are famous for being laughed at. So I support scientists and mathematicians. My special interest is the calendar. This tells me the day and time of year, so my nobles know when to order peasants to plant their crops. I met some very interesting Arab mathematicians when I went on Crusade in the Middle East. I must invite them to my palace.*

Oh dear.

I ALWAYS LISTEN TO MY ASTROLOGERS AND DOCTORS. *My astrological calendars show the positions of the stars. I pay for the best astrologers to study these, then tell me the state of my health. If I am a little weak, then I will ask the doctor to release some of my blood. Bloodletting makes me feel MUCH better. So does all that expensive fussing over ME.*

Fiendish Fact File

- The king could enter any house in his kingdom, stay at the host's expense, and take whatever he wanted.

- Peasants entertained themselves with ball games such as early tennis or football. Balls were made of animal bladders or pieces of cloth wound and stitched tightly.

I'm a Really Fussy Eater

Shall I just go and set the table dear?

A king simply cannot do his duties on an empty stomach. So his kitchens are very important, and I'm very proud of mine. My travels for the Crusades have given me a taste of exciting new flavors, from Persian fruits in the Middle East to spices from Zanzibar Island off the East African coast.

I INSIST THAT MY WIFE HELPS WITH THE MENU. The good Queen went with me on one of my Crusades and came back with new ingredients, recipes, and manners. Thanks to her, my Great Hall is lined with silk tapestries.

GOOD TABLE MANNERS ARE VITAL. I always sit at the main table on a raised platform, with the most important nobles and guests next to me. The other tables are very long and are covered with wooden planks holding the buffet banquet. People seated the farthest from me are the least important—and they know it. I insist that everyone washes their hands first and uses gold and silver knives and spoons. I believe my peasants eat with iron knives and wooden spoons. So be it.

See? If you do exactly as I say, you can sit at the top table.

ONLY THE BEST FOOD WILL DO. My guests are delighted when the servers bring on the jelly starters in the shape of birds. How they laugh and clap! The tables then fill up with dishes of spiced meat, from pigeon and peacock to cuckoo and crow. Pies dripping with fruit, honey, and rosewater finish the meal off. Oh, those apricots and pomegranates! Those luscious peaches! Quick! Where's my taster? He tries all my food first, just in case it's poisoned.

MY SIMPLE PEASANTS MUST EAT SIMPLE FOODS. I approve of rye and barley bread as they fill my peasants' stomachs and help them work hard. They seem to eat a lot of vegetables, from cabbages and carrots to leeks and lentils—all cooked into a thick potage, or soup. Horrid! Peasants pluck wild cherries, strawberries, and damsons, as well as nuts. Strangely, peasants' skin looks really lovely. It must be all that toiling in the open air. Or could it be the fresh fruit and vegetables? Surely not.

Poison ivy. Here, have some, My Lord King!

Pssst! What's the secret of your healthy skin?

Fiendish Fact File

- The oldest known medieval cookbook is from the twelfth century. It was found in Durham Cathedral in England. It includes recipes for medicines and ointments.

- Water was impure, so people drank weak ale and cider. The alcohol and boiling needed to make them helped kill bacteria.

My Royal Death

I plan my funeral to the last detail. My Queen is from another country and says that some of her customs must be included in the ceremony too. This is what happens when we marry to gain influence and territory abroad. Sadly, my wishes may not be followed, especially if there is a fight to inherit the throne.

Tear up his funeral wish list! I'm in charge now.

IF I DIE IN BATTLE I WILL BE BURIED IN MY BEST SUIT OF ARMOR. It will not be new. The Black Prince (1330–1376), of Wales and French Aquitaine, was buried in a used suit of armor. If that was good enough for him, it's good enough for me! If I die at home, the Queen will dress me in my finest clothes and a crown. My hands will be crossed over like the Christian cross. My open casket will be covered with a decorated cloth.

They've put me in cheap shoes!

I INSIST THAT ALL MY NOBLES SHOW UP. My knights will accompany my casket, dressed in full shining armor. Bishops will walk beside my body, and hooded monks will chant prayers over me. Banners bearing my royal crest will wave as my subjects, all forced to wear black, wail and faint. Hopefully.

MY BODY WILL BE BURIED IN A STONE TOMB IN MY BIGGEST CATHEDRAL. Some kings have other ideas. Robert the Bruce of Scotland (1274-1329) wanted his heart to be buried in Jerusalem. It was carried in a silver casket as far as Spain but never quite made it to the Holy Land. You can't have everything you want when you die, even if you're king.

Fiendish Fact File

- Hundreds of plague victims were buried together in mass graves. Plague, or the Black Death, killed more than one-third of the medieval European population.

- Henry I of England (1068-1135) was buried in Reading Abbey in England, but his internal organs lie in Rouen Cathedral, France.

I WILL NOT CHOOSE AN UNDIGNIFIED BURIAL. How unfortunate for Richard III of England (1452-1485)! He fought valiantly at the Battle of Bosworth Field in 1485 but was slain by Henry Tudor (1457-1509). Henry's troops buried his body on the battlefield. Worse, they dug it up again, dragged it to a different hole, and dumped it. My astrologers tell me that way in the future, Richard III will be found underneath a parking lot—whatever that may be. But I know I will not suffer that fate. I'm so brilliant, I'll probably be made a saint. Long live ME!

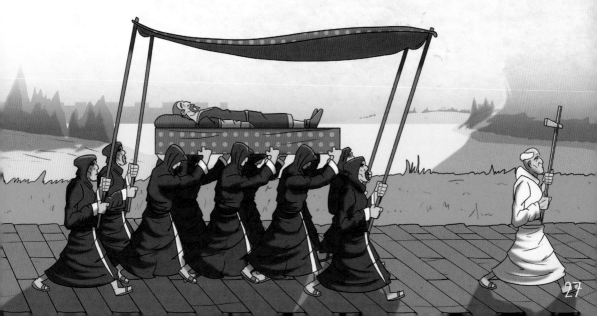

Chivalry—the Medieval Knightly Code

Kings and knights fought and plotted against each other. But they also had to follow a code of behavior called chivalry. The twelfth and thirteenth centuries were the most chivalrous times.

GUARDING WEAPONS

A king's and lord's young squire gained his knighthood in a ceremony. To prepare, he had to guard his weapons all night long in a church, which was a chivalrous discipline.

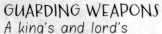

FASTING ALL NIGHT

In the morning, having eaten nothing, the young squire took a bath. He put on a long, white robe and confessed his sins. He was given his swords and javelin, which were blessed by a priest.

VOWS OF CHIVALRY

A knight swore to defend the holy church and respect priests. He made these promises in front of godfathers, who made sure that the knight kept his vows.

28

SEEKING DANGEROUS CHALLENGES

A knight had to tackle opponents with valor, honor, and pride. He had to accept his king's challenges too. He dueled with anyone who insulted him or his king.

LEADING FROM THE FRONT

As a leader, a knight's lance was decorated with a banner of his coat of arms. He was unchivalrous if he aimed his lance below his opponent's belt.

THE MEANING OF CHIVALRY

The word comes from *chevalerie*, an old French word for "knights on horseback" (*cheval* means "horse" in French). Then it came to mean fighting with honorable or "chivalrous" rules.

CHIVALROUS LOVE

Eleanor of Aquitaine established the Court of Love in Poitiers, France. It attracted poets, musicians, and artists, who created rules on chivalrous or courtly love.

GALLANT BEHAVIOR

Knights, princes, and kings adopted Eleanor's idea of courtly love. A chivalrous man played music to his desired woman, wrote poems for her, and sometimes fought for her.

Ten More Fiendish Kings

Here are some more fiendish medieval kings. I hope you will agree that they are not as fiendish as me.

1 Boleslaw the Brave of Poland (reigned 992–1025) gained 748 miles (1204 kilometers) of territory stretching from Ukraine to Germany. On the way he blinded the Bohemian king and burned the German town of Strehla, capturing its citizens.

2 Sviatopolk the Cursed, Grand Prince of Kiev (reigned 1015–1019) murdered his rival brothers, Gleb and Boris. He had their bodies dragged into the woods where they rotted for thirty years. He spent his reign brutally fending off armies from Russia.

3 Olaf II Haraldsson of Norway (reigned 1016–1030) was also known as Saint Olaf. But he started off as a Viking gang leader, plundering the shores of northern Europe. Then he took over an empty throne in west Norway and fought to unite the country.

4 William Duke of Normandy became King of England (reigned 1066–1087) after defeating King Harold at the Battle of Hastings. He burned crops, homes, and livestock to stop rebellions. In Alençon, France, William cut off the hands and feet of anyone who mocked him for being the grandson of a tanner.

5 John I of England (reigned 1199–1216) tried to sieze the throne from his brother, Richard the Lionheart, while he was away fighting. He starved twenty-two rebel knights to death, taxed the people heavily, and tortured those who could not pay.

6 Pedro the Cruel of Castile and Leon, Spain (reigned 1350–1369), *invited his half brother, Fadrique, to dinner at his palace in Seville in 1358. Then Fadrique's skull was smashed and his courtiers were murdered. Pedro calmly sat down to dinner with Fadrique's body still on the floor.*

7 Sigismund of Bohemia (reigned 1419–1437) *put his peaceful half brother, Wenceslas IV of Bohemia in prison twice. Sigismund also allowed a great religious thinker, Jan Hus, to be burned at the stake.*

8 Vlad III (the Impaler), Prince of Romania (reigned 1448–1476), *hid rows of sharpened sticks that speared thousands of advancing enemy troops. Then he left them to die. He invited hundreds of his nobles to a banquet at his castle then had them murdered and their bodies stuck on spikes.*

9 Duke Cesare Borgia of Valentinois (1498–1507) *Did Cesare cut his brother's throat and dump him in the River Tiber in Italy? Probably. This duke was a Roman Catholic cardinal who became a fiendish knight.*

10 Ferdinand of Aragon *and his wife, Isabella of Castile (reigned 1479–1516), united Spain. But they also set up the Inquisition, which persecuted non-Catholic Christians and condemned them to torture, banishment, or being burned at the stake.*

INDEX

The Author

Catherine Chambers was born in Adelaide, South Australia, and brought up in England. She earned a degree in African History and Swahili at the School of Oriental and African Studies, London. Catherine has written about 130 titles for children and young adults, mainly non-fiction, and she enjoys seeking out intriguing facts for her non-fiction titles.

The Illustrator

Ryan Pentney lives and works in Norwich, in the United Kingdom. Growing up in the 1990s, he was surrounded by iconic cartoons, comics, and books that have remained a passion with him. Inspired by these childhood heroes as well as more modern works, Ryan creates his own characters and stories in the hope of inspiring the next generation. He uses the latest technology and traditional techniques to make stylized digital artworks